Sisterfriends

Words of Encouragement, Enlightenment and Empowerment from one Sister to another.

Volume I

Diretha:
Blessing + Peace!
Linda Willis

Edited by Linda Willis and Dr. Harold Taylor.

How to contact the author of this book:
Linda Willis
Riverside Missionary Baptist Church
3560 South Third Street
Memphis, Tennessee 38109
Or email her at: Sister1380@aol.com
For reorders of *Sisterfriends*
Write Linda Willis at the above address, or call
901-789-4570 or 901-785-9620

First printing 1999
Second printing 2003

Riverside Printing
2519 Summer Avenue
Memphis,TN 38112

Sisterfriends

ISBN #1-893555-09-7
Copyright by Linda Willis, 1999

Printed in the U.S.A.

Dedication

I wish to dedicate this booklet to my wonderful husband, Kevin B. Willis, Sr., to my adorable children, Kelli and Kevin, Jr. and to all of my

Sisterfriends

who are always there to cheer me on!

Table of Contents

To My Sisterfriends . . .

As women, we have so many experiences in common. Many of us have experienced the expectation of a relationship, the joys of motherhood, and the excitement of success. Likewise, we also share the pain of rejection, the fear of failure, the anxiety of change, and the disappointment of a lost dream. For some of us the deep dark abyss of depression becomes our home. Someone once said that the definition of insanity is trying the exact same thing over and over expecting to get a different result. That definition would certainly qualify most of us for a mental institution. I can definitely speak for myself, and say that I was on my way to insanity. When my life was in turmoil, I continued to try the same methods for solving my problems that had not worked, expecting them to work the next time. I tried to hide my problems and act as if everything was okay.

Hallelujah to a God who looks beyond our faults and recognizes our needs! He sent a virtuous woman across my path who became a refuge for my weak soul. She gave me what only another *Sisterfriend* can give, sisterly love.

From her life God planted a seed in my heart for my *Sisterfriends*. My compassion and concern causes me to want to share with women from all walks of life. You see, I survived my crisis and came out strong and victorious. But I can't really be free knowing that I have left others behind. I want to share some wisdom and encouragement with my *Sisterfriends*. I'm so excited about this opportunity. I believe that within the lessons learned through my challenges and struggles, there are definite blessings awaiting you!

Vision

Without a vision, the people perish (Proverbs. 29:18). This scripture is not just relative to congregations of people, but to individuals likewise. It is so easy to find yourself without a vision. I found myself at this point in my life three years ago. I was very busy being a wife and a mother, making sure that everyone had what they needed. When it came to thoughts of the future, my thoughts were always about what my children were going to become, and where God was going to take my husband in the ministry. I am not exactly sure when I noticed this, but I began feeling that something was wrong. And as I am accustomed to doing, I began soul-searching. I found that I had become so consumed with everyone else's life, that I did not have one of my own. I am not suggesting that being a good wife and mother is not important, because it is. But when we neglect ourselves in the process, things become unbalanced. If you are not careful, you find yourself with low self-esteem and with feelings of resentment and frustration. I know, because I did! I was perishing because I did not have a vision. I was existing day to day, without any expectations for my future. I was created with purpose, but I was not pursuing it. Revelation concerning who I was to become had ceased. When you do not have a vision, you wander aimlessly through life, only bumping into success. God wants us to live intentionally, to pursue life in Him and all that it has to offer. He wants us to live victoriously, striving to conquer, not waiting to be ambushed.

Today, you may be where I was three years ago. You are coping with feelings of low self-worth, frustration, resentment and bitterness. You may even be bound by depression. You admire the accomplishments of others, but haven't thought of the possibility of great things happening in your own life. Only you can change your situation. Now is a good time to make that change. God declares in Jeremiah 29:11, *For I know the thoughts that I think toward you, saith the Lord, thoughts of peace, and not evil, to give you an expected end.*

Self-Esteem

Self-esteem is the value given to oneself as a result of personal assessment. It is the attitude you have toward yourself. Now before you pat yourself on the back for having high self-esteem, let's take a closer look.

Self-esteem is determined by how you feel about you before anything is added. It is what you think of yourself without the weave, the nail tips, and the designer clothes. It is who you feel you are without a title or a degree. Self-esteem is who you are when your friends are few and companionship is scarce. It is the value given to the original you!

I believe that you can't have relationships with others until you have a healthy relationship with yourself. It is impossible to have a healthy relationship with yourself if you don't like you. When you don't like your breasts because they're too small, or too large; the color of your skin is too light, or too dark; your hair too thin or your legs too small, you become your own worst enemy. Loving yourself requires that you love you... just as you are.

There are those of you whose self-esteem wavers, not because of your looks, but because of your experiences. As little girls, some of you were molested, raped, and emotionally abused. You have been left with inner scars that make you feel unworthy and ashamed. As teenagers, some of you were just down right disobedient and did things that you now regret.

Maybe you had a baby out of wedlock; had so many sexual partners that you are too ashamed to count them; or did drugs and everything else that was out there to do. If your list is long or short, it is okay. What matters is who you are, not what you have done.

How do you build self-esteem? You've got to stop putting yourself down. Sit down in front of the mirror and begin a new relationship with you. Introduce yourself to who you are on the inside. Remind yourself of how special you are. Appreciate your body, it's the only one you have. Rejoice over your successes and laugh at your mistakes. Forgive yourself for time wasted and forget about opportunities missed. Believe in yourself and become your greatest supporter. Most of all, thank God for His wisdom. He knew exactly what He was doing when He created you!

Faith

What have you decided about your situation? Have you determined that you can't win? Have you just accepted that it is more than you can handle? Chances are you have not been using your shield of faith. The Bible tells us that the shield of faith blocks the fiery darts of the enemy. He uses penetrating suggestions of fear and failure to fill our minds (the true battleground) with worry, anxiety, and ultimately defeat. Sister, defeat can not come until it is allowed to be established in your mind. When you shield yourself with faith in an all-powerful God, no enemy can overtake you.

So, before you hammer the last nail into the coffin or before you file spiritual bankruptcy, flex your faith one more time. I am not talking about just hanging on one more day, but a total resurgence of spiritual energy. I am talking about a realization of who you are in Christ.

It has been said, *Heat makes things rise.* Well if the pressure is on in your life, rise to the occasion. Stop repeating what everybody else is saying about your outcome and say what God says, *No weapon formed against you will prosper.* Start believing in your heart that God is not a man that He should lie. His word will not return to Him void, but will accomplish what He desires and achieve the purpose for which it was sent. Begin to realize faith without works is dead. Therefore, take a radical stand for the outcome you desire. When it's your last shot, you've got to give it all you've got. You have to do the unthinkable, look for the unexpected, and speak the unexplainable in order to receive the impossible. What do you have to lose? Who do you have to impress? *Sisterfriend,* stand up in faith!

Too Hard?

Is anything too hard for God? This question had to be answered when I reached the end of my rope and found no knot. There comes a time in our lives when we realize our limitations. Our ability to tie a knot and hang on is found in our belief that nothing is too hard for God. Sister, when you have tried everything and are mentally and physically drained . . . Just before you give up, Look UP! Remind yourself that nothing is too hard for God. Encourage yourself by knowing that God sees your situation. Motivate yourself by believing that faith without works is dead. Whether it is a relationship that's gone bad, children who have gone astray, or plans that are not working out, you are not experiencing a problem that God has not solved before. Our responsibility is to walk by faith.

Free

Sisterfriend, it is a tragedy for people to walk around in bondage behind invisible bars of guilt and shame. But the greater tragedy is for those who are unbound, unchained, and free, to continue to live behind those bars of guilt and shame. They are ignorant to the fact that the door is unlocked, the bars are open, and the chain has been broken. Jesus tells us, *You shall know the truth, and the truth shall make you free.* Someone recently asked me, *How do you know when you are free?* Well this is the way I answered this question:

I am a native of Dallas, Texas where African Americans celebrate a holiday fondly called ***Juneteenth.*** On January 1, 1863, Abraham Lincoln signed the Emancipation Proclamation that freed the slaves. But it wasn't until the 19th of June in 1865 that the Black slaves in Texas got the news. Thus our Independence Day became June 19th.

Well, how do you know when you have been set free? It is when truth travels beyond your circumstances; beyond your disappointments, beyond your heartache, and beyond even your own flesh. It's when truth gives your spirit the news that your Emancipation Proclamation was signed over 2,000 years ago by a Savior named Jesus Christ, in red blood on an old wooden cross. The truth is that Christ has redeemed you from bondage. And now God accepts you as you are, because you are covered in Christ's righteousness. When your *spirit* gets this news and you begin walking in this liberty you will know that you are free.

One Step

As I was reading a book from one of my favorite authors, I read something that I thought was most powerful. The author said, *No matter how many steps are between you and God, He will make all but one.*

Sisterfriend, I can't think of a greater truth that needs to be embraced. This one truth gave me a greater understanding of how much God really loves me, and the lengths He will take to pursue a closer relationship with me. It said to me that His desire is that there would be no distance between us. It suggested to me that there is an opportunity to be so close to Him, that I can hear Him when He whispers. Herein lies the deeper truth. If you and I could hear Him clearly, we would understand the purpose for our lives and fulfill our destiny. If we could somehow hear Him when He calls, we could stay focused and not make so many mistakes. If we could just be near Him to hear when He whispers, we would receive the promises of victory and life everlasting.

The other part of this truth is that there is *a step* that we must make. God will make 99, but we must put forth the effort to make one. As you begin assessing the steps that need to be taken to make your life better, know that there is one step that would make all of your other steps successful. That is the step toward Him!

Unmask

There is a movement in our society today toward comfort and ease. This has caused a great temptation in the life of Christians to believe that the abundant life means a life without trouble. We now frown upon those who find themselves experiencing trials as if they are not true Christians. Something must be wrong with their relationship with God. Everybody has to come to Sunday service wearing their *every-thing-is-perfect-in-my-life* mask.

Sisterfriend, it is time for us to unmask! It is time for us to stop being embarrassed and ashamed. I am not suggesting that you go out and tell everybody your business, nor am I saying that you must wear sorrow on your face. I am speaking of liberation from the opinions of others. Opinions that causes us to go into hiding or to live in denial.

Sisterfriend, there is nothing new under the sun. Whatever problem you are having, somebody else has had it too. It does not necessarily mean you aren't living right, it could be that your number has come up on the enemy's hit list. But as the saying goes, *The devil meant it for evil, but God meant it for good.* So go ahead, turn that trial into a testimony. Turn your shame into a sacrifice of praise, and your embarrassment into edification for someone else. You will be amazed at how many people you will bless!

Confront

Sisterfriend, the first step to taking off your *every-thing-is-perfect-in-my-life* mask is to confront the situation at hand. You must come out of hiding, and stop living in denial. You must make a decision to walk through the problem. No one enjoys experiencing pain or hardship, but if you are going to come out, you must go through. Closing yourself up in the house will not make it go away, neither does burying yourself in work, make it disappear!

The Apostle Paul says that we must endure hardship as a good soldier. When the orders are given, whether in the cold of winter, or the heat of summer, soldiers must go. So it is with us. God orders our steps, and we must go through. Have you ever wondered, *Why now, Lord? Just when it looked as if everything was going well.* Have you ever said, *Lord, give me anything but this?* But the truth is, if God left it up to us, we would never experience trouble! So in His omniscience, He chooses our path and schedules our struggles. *Sister-friend,* I hope it will encourage you to know that He also decides the appointed time of our deliverance.

The Right Thing

Another area that we should consider when we are facing difficult situations in our lives is how we treat those involved. I am no stranger to difficult situations or people. Just like anybody else, I have wanted to pay someone back for mistreating me. No matter how holy we profess to be, we all have that instinct to attack when we feel violated. However, we are more than instinctive beings. We have been created with a consciousness (an awareness) of right and wrong. God wants us to use this awareness as a means to choose to do the right thing. Two wrongs have never made anything right. I believe I have made some bad situations worse by reacting wrongly to them.

Sisterfriend, doing the right thing begins with pure motives. This has to do with what is in our heart. We have to get rid of the desire to prove a point or get revenge. These desires, when carried out, lower us to the level of the other person. The only thing that has been proven when we lower ourselves to the malicious level of another, is the power they have over us.

What can you do instead, when dealing with a difficult person? Jesus says, *Love your enemies, do good to those who hate you, bless those who curse you, pray for those who mistreat you. Do to others as you would have them do to you. Sisterfriend*, this really works! Love has a way of disarming the most difficult person, and prayer does change things. *Sisterfriend,* our purpose for doing the right thing is not just to disarm difficult people, but to please God in all that we do. I hold fast to the thought that when our ways please God,

He will make even our enemies to be at peace with us. We will not only be at peace with our enemies, but we will be able to sleep at night because we will be at peace with ourselves.

Motherhood

Motherhood is an awesome responsibility with only one chance to get it right. There are no rehearsals or retakes. You do the best you can do, with the knowledge that you have, and pray that you are doing something right. Even with doing it right, there are no guarantees. It is by the grace of God that our children succeed.

Sisterfriend, I think that it is a pity that mothers are celebrated only one day out of the year. Secretaries get a whole week, and African American History gets a month. Think about it . . . there would be no secretaries to appreciate without mothers and no African American history to celebrate, if it wasn't for the strength and determination of mothers.

Well, from one mother to another, I salute you. Because I know the challenges you face, being a nurturer, and the love that you demonstrate as a caregiver; I appreciate you. I know the power you possess as the hand that rocks the cradle, and I know the wisdom that you have as matriarchs of society. I honor you today, and every day.

Rain

Do you remember the saying, "April showers bring May flowers?" It reminds us that not only does a plant need sunshine to make it grow, it also needs rain. Although rain is an inconvenience to us, it is God's way of providing a necessary nutrient to the earth. Even in our lives, *Sisterfriend,* we need some rain to help us grow. Our lives would dry up and die from complacency and stagnation if every day was sunny. The storms of life we go through serve as showers of experience that give us wisdom and determination. Each trial presents an opportunity for us to grow in character and strength.

Rain not only waters the earth, but it also cleanses it. Likewise, those tears we shed act as cleansing agents to rid our souls of emotional pollutants of anger, hatred, anxiety and frustration. Crying allows us to become vulnerable to the elements of life called pain and sorrow. Tears wash away our pride, and self will. All of us could use this kind of cleansing!

Sisterfriend, if you are experiencing a rainy season in your life, if it seems as if a torrential downpour is flooding your existence, know that growth is on the way. The rain has not come to drown you, but to water the seed of your life so that you will grow.

A Cold Snap

Last week we experienced an unexpected change in weather that threw us all for a loop. This *cold snap* as my mother would call it, came after the flowers began to bloom, trees began to bud, and we began to shed our winter clothes. Just when we thought winter was over, we found ourselves experiencing freezing temperatures and snow flurries. The only consolation I could find was in knowing that this was a temporary condition, spring would definitely come.

Sisterfriend, like the trees, you may have started to bud. You started making steps toward improving your life. Maybe you were coming out of debt, had lost seven of those 20 pounds, or had packed Johnny No-Good's clothes. Some of you finally cleaned out your emotional closets and began working toward your dreams. You thought you had made it through your winter. And just when you got the courage to spring forth, a cold snap occurred. *A cold snap* in life is anything that takes you two steps backwards just after you've made one step forward. Sometimes it is a door closed in your face, a lack of support from loved ones, or you simply fell off the wagon.

Life is like nature, it goes in cycles. In the midst of whatever has caused your setback, you must believe that it's temporary. Remember, we do not throw away our summer clothing when winter comes, we only pack them away. Don't throw away your goals and dreams. You may have to pack them away for a moment but they are too valuable to discard. *Never make permanent decisions based on a temporary circumstances.* If you are experiencing a cold snap in your life, hang on, spring is coming!

Fear

As you know, gusty winds are typical for the month of March. The other day, I came out of the hair salon with my hair freshly done and intact. Before I could get to the car, the wind had blown it all out of place. While driving, I even found myself clutching the steering wheel trying to keep my car steady as the violent winds blew. This brought to mind a sermon my husband preached concerning fear.

He said that the spirit of fear is like the wind. It is a powerful force that you cannot see. When it blows in our lives, it wreaks havoc.

Sisterfriend, fear has the power to throw things in your life out of place. Your confidence, self-esteem, and determination can be tossed around as the leaves that are blown from one yard to another. Things that you know you can do and goals that you can achieve, can become torn and tattered by a sudden gust of fear. Like the wind kicks up dust, and impairs your ability to see, fear also kicks up anxiety and doubt that hinders your ability to believe. If you don't hold on tightly to what is in your heart, you will find yourself blown off course.

Sisterfriend, when you experience the violent wind of fear tossing you to and fro, when the dust of anxiety and doubt is flying and you cannot see your way clearly; cling to the Word of God, and let faith be your guide. Realize that like the month of March, the wind of fear is typical of this time in our life . . . it will pass. The Bible tells us, God has not given us *a spirit of fear,* but of power, love and sound mind. Know that God has given you the power to hang on, love to keep you secure, and a sound mind to see your way through.

Fractions

As I talk with women who are single, I find that some view themselves as *fractions*. *Fractions* are sisters who feel incomplete without a man, and spend most of their time looking for him. They believe that whatever is lacking in their lives will be found in a relationship. Some sisters will not take a vacation, enjoy a sunset, or even a dinner if not accompanied by

Mr. Right. Well, my Sister, if this describes you, it is time to release the *hold button* in your life. Desiring companionship is a natural feeling, but if you are waiting for *Mr. Right* so that you can finally be complete, you have missed him. God is the only one who can do for you what you cannot do for yourself. He designed relationships to compliment us, not complete us.

Codependent

Do you feel responsible for other people's feelings, actions, needs, and destiny? Do you feel compelled to help people solve their problems? Do you get upset when your help is not effective? Do you wonder why people don't do the same for you? You could be Codependent. A Codependent person is one who gets consumed with another person's well-being, to the point of trying to control their actions. At that point, the person has stepped into sickness themselves.

Sisterfriend, most of us fit this description. Whether it is our husband, significant other, children, or friend, there is usually someone in our lives that we are trying to control by helping them. The problem occurs when helping them, hurts us. All of us know someone who has great potential but continues to make bad choices. The great potential that we see, drives us overboard in trying to help them. But the truth is that good potential is going to stay right where it is, *in* them, until they want it to come out. An added truth is that there are a whole lot of folk who need help, but Sister, they have to want it. As the saying goes, *God helps those who help themselves.*

Why raise this issue? Because as women, our natural inclination is to be caretakers. We give until it is gone! We love until it hurts! Please don't misunderstand me, I believe in helping. I am just learning from my mistakes. I acknowledge the fact that sometimes I have made myself sick with worry and anxiety over things that were happening in someone else's life. But I respectfully acknowledge today, that I don't have the power, nor the right to control someone else's life. I choose not to be codependent. My heart will be saddened by their choices but it is their life to live.

Love

Love is...

The end of this statement is being completed everyday of our lives. It is shown in how we treat others as well as ourselves. Through love God gives us the unique opportunity to express what is divine on a human level. I can not think of anything more heavenly than the relationship between a man and a woman. Words cannot describe it when it is right, because it was not made on earth. God did it!

Sisterfriend, what do you think love is? I believe love is whatever someone needs that you can give. Love is the least expensive present you can give and the most valuable gift you can receive. It can be a warm smile, words of encouragement, some understanding, a little personal space, or a whole lot of affection. When given, love is the most powerful, life-changing gift one can experience. I know because my life was changed twelve years ago when God gave me love wrapped up in Kevin Willis, my husband. Kevin's love has been whatever I needed, that he had. It has given life to two beautiful children, produced strength to overcome life's struggles, patience to handle our differences, and kindness to make it all worthwhile.

Precious Moments

In recognition of Black History month, I had my daughter to check out library books on African American women. One day as I combed her hair, she shared with me her feelings about the stories she had read. She was troubled by the injustices that were endured by the women she read about. I took this opportunity to help her understand that she had come from a rich heritage of women. Women who withstood the tremendous struggles of racism to give her freedom. I explained how those women fought overwhelming battles of sexism to give her an opportunity to make her own choices. It was because of those women, she could now excel as far as her mind will take her. I further admonished that she had an obligation to take advantage of the privileges now available to her so that their labor would not be in vain.

Suddenly, I remembered being a little girl, hearing my mother say the same things to me as she combed my hair. I could hear the words emanating from my own mother's voice: _You can be anything you want to be. The way has already been paved._ Those words inspired me more than any text book. They have lived with me to this very day.

Sisterfriend, what an opportunity God gives us as mothers. He allows us to empower the next generation for excellence. I hope you will use those precious moments with your _Little Sisterfriends,_ to share the powerful legacy of their ancestry. This is your opportunity to speak into their lives, and inspire them to achieve greatness.

Truth

Whenever I am facing a difficult situation, the first thing I ask God is that He would open my eyes that I may see truth. I want to be able to distinguish between what is right and wrong, and what is permanent and what is temporary. These distinctions may seem simple but when facing complex situations our judgment can be clouded. Right begins to look wrong and wrong starts looking right. It is easy to find ourselves mixing truth with feelings, and facts with opinions. Truth is not founded upon feelings, nor is it based upon opinions. *Sisterfriend*, I can honestly say that I have foolishly allowed myself to become depressed and filled with anxiety over things that were just temporary. I got off the pathway of truth, and traveled down the road of false assumptions. I assumed a delay was a denial and a closed door was a locked door.

Feelings of hopelessness will overcome you if you do not keep your eyes focused on truth. And what about opinions? Everyone can tell you what they would do if they were you, but the truth is, they are not. You have to seek an understanding of your situation from God. He proclaims that He is Truth. Everything in your life must be measured according to His word. *Sisterfriend,* when you walk in truth it stabilizes your mind, and allows you to make sound decisions. It enhances your ability to receive direction from God, therefore, creating an atmosphere for your deliverance.

A Distorted Design

A well-known magazine published an article that grappled with a God who could allow women to endure the atrocities of sexual abuse by predators, relatives, and even their own fathers. I wanted to speak to this issue in hopes of bringing some help and healing to those who are asking this question.

Women throughout history have been victimized by those who through the vehicle of sex, have stolen their purity, possessions, and peace of mind. Consequently, many women have a marred view of sexuality based on their painful experiences. It is often difficult to understand where God is in all of this. But we must make the distinction between God and His creation. It has been mankind that has distorted what God purposed to be *good*. This should not come as a surprise because mankind has had a proclivity to destroy everything God made, including one another, since the days of Adam and Eve. This abuse of something that God intended to be beautiful has left women feeling guilty, ashamed, isolated, and worthless.

But to really know the real purpose of something, we must go back to it's original design. God not only designed sex to allow us to become co-creators with Him in the producing of offspring, but He designed the coming together of man and woman physically to provide mutual gratification, and express the highest level of intimacy between two people.

Has this design been distorted? Yes. But the Bible says *you shall know the truth and the truth shall make you free*. I want some woman today, to be made free by knowing the truth. Free to disconnect the meaning of intimacy from the painful experience of sexual abuse.

Free to put blame in its rightful place. Free to appreciate the characteristics of her femininity. Free to own her own desires and passions and free to know the feeling of oneness through physical intimacy.

Sleepless Nights

In our efforts to fix our lives and the people in them, we often find ourselves experiencing sleepless nights. Our focus on what is not right and what is not working out, leaves little room for noticing what is. Being blessed is not just a matter of getting what we want, but also appreciating what we have. Life, health, and a sound mind are blessings that get overlooked because of the despair over our desires. However, without these blessings all others would be useless. *Sisterfriend*, I encourage you to take a moment to breathe, relax and focus on the good, instead of the bad. Chances are you will end your nights counting blessings instead of sheep.

God's Will

Have you ever found yourself truly seeking God's will for your life? I have. You know how it is when you really want to do the right thing.

While reading my Bible one day, I discovered a scripture that says, *In everything give thanks, for this is the will of God in Christ Jesus concerning you.* God's will for my life was right there, spelled out in black and white. *Give thanks.* How simple, yet profound. God's will for my life is a position, not a purpose.

He is concerned about my attitude; not my altitude. He desires that I have an attitude of gratitude toward Him. In every situation, I am to give thanks. Most of us do not have a problem with being thankful for the good experiences, but what about the bad? This is our true challenge in accepting God's will for us to give thanks in everything.

What is there to be thankful about in tragedy, hurt and pain? *Sisterfriend,* God's will is that we look deeper into those not-so-good experiences, and see Him. Our thankfulness comes in that He is there. Even when we do not know it, He is there. Whether we allow His presence to comfort us during these times, is our choice, but He is there. Thanksgiving should be every day, for this is the will of God in Christ Jesus concerning you.

Loneliness

As I sat down to write you today, I begin to think about those who are experiencing loneliness. While many people are anxiously awaiting the end of the day, others face it with dread. Some of you will have an empty seat at the dinner table tonight. Some of you find it hard to live up to the expectations of others. I realize it is difficult to act happy when you are hurting on the inside. I am not talking about physical pain . . . I am speaking of the emotional agony of loneliness and despair.

I was sharing on this week with a lady whose husband died earlier this year. She questioned whether she was abnormal because she was still grieving his death. I replied, *I don't believe that anyone can decide what is the proper amount of time to grieve over someone with whom you spent 43 years of your life.*

I do know that God sent His Son to heal the brokenhearted and if you will submit yourself to Him, He will soothe your sorrows. I also understand that some of you will be lonely because you don't have that *special someone* in your life. Maybe it is due to a relationship that did not work out or you just haven't found what you are looking for.

So much advice is given on how to handle this difficult time. Some will tell you to keep yourself busy, others advise to share your feelings with a friend. I'm not going to tell you what I think you should do, instead, I would like to tell you what I am going to do. I am going to lift you up before God daily, in my prayers. I don't know who you are, but God knows. I am not just telling you this because it sounds good to say. I am saying this because you are my *Sisterfriend,* and I care. I cannot cure your loneliness, neither can I heal your pain, but I can pray to the One who can. I believe the power of God can help you overcome every challenge that you face. So in the upcoming days, when nights become long, and the days are difficult, if you begin to feel like you just cannot make it, remember you've got a *Sisterfriend* who is praying for you.

Cloud

On a recent trip, I glanced out of the window of the airplane and saw clouds that looked like glimpses of heaven. When we landed and departed the plane, I looked into the sky and saw the storm clouds. As I reflected on this experience, I thought about how many times I had judged life based on where I was sitting. With the clouds, one moment I saw glimpses of heaven and felt peace, and the next moment I saw storm clouds, and felt fear. *Sisterfriend,* just like the airplane . . . we have the ability to *ride* above the clouds. We can see problems as challenges, dead ends as turning points, and difficult people as opportunities to give love. Make a decision today about the clouds in your life. They can either be your vision of a glorious future, or your sign of a future storm.

Happy Birthday

Recently I celebrated my birthday. The celebration was not one with balloons, food and friends. It was more of a mental party with all my experiences as guests. For the first time, I could handle seeing them all together. The good experiences, the bad, and the ones that hurt had all come to celebrate this year of growth with me. This was really special for them because they all finally felt welcomed. You see, I used to only want to remember the good times. The bad were too embarrassing and the ones that hurt were too painful. As we began to reminisce, I could appreciate them all. The good experiences had given me the much needed spurts of joy and happiness that I needed to maintain self-worth and feel loved. The bad experiences had developed in me patience, determination and courage. The ones that hurt had produced strength, compassion, and most of all the ability to forgive. I could see that they had made me the person I am today.

Another person attended my celebration, the most important guest of all. The Holy Spirit was present as always. His voice could be heard above all the rest. He said, *My child, none of these experiences could have happened had I not allowed them. I opened the door of your life and decided who would come in. They have all been working together for your good. Through them, I have been able to give you your most valuable asset, wisdom. I have given you a discerning heart to travel beneath the surface, to see truth. I have given you the ability to apply what you have learned so that you will exercise righteousness.* Then He gave me some future instructions from His word from Proverbs 4:6:

Do not forsake wisdom, and she will protect you; love her, and she will watch over you. Wisdom is supreme therefore get wisdom. Though it cost all you have, get understanding. Esteem her, and she will exalt you; embrace her, and she will honor you. She will set a garland of grace on your head, and present you with a crown of splendor.

They all wished me happy birthday and left, except for one, the Holy Spirit. He is my constant companion. I will forever cherish this celebration, it was the most meaningful party I ever had.

Sisterfriend, today does not have to be your birthday for you to have this wonderful celebration. Some of you know, because you have had your own. This celebration takes place whenever you are ready to embrace life. How much time have we spent running from our past, trying to escape our present and avoiding our future. _Sisterfriend_, the ultimate truth is that until the day you die, your life will always consist of a past, present, and future. The powerful revelation in this is that God designed it that way to bring His purpose forth in your life. These three phases are constantly rotating in your life to grow you in wisdom. Can you hear the Psalmist saying, _Lord teach us to number our days, that we may apply our hearts unto wisdom?_ Every tear that you have cried, every heartache

you have felt, every friend that stabbed you in the back, every man that did you wrong, every plan that did not work, and every moment of happiness that you have experienced, has had wisdom wrapped inside of it. Did you get it? If so, throw a party! Invite another *Sister-friend* if you want, she needs to celebrate too. Now that my mascara is running down my face, and I feel a dance in my feet, I better move on.

Pregnant

The story of the Virgin Mary and the immaculate conception has been told a million times. It recounts the moment in history when God chose a humble young woman to birth the Savior of the world. However, this story actually is about more than one woman. It speaks of every woman who is pregnant with potential. This divine pregnancy is the abilities, passions and talents waiting to be delivered from the womb of every *Sisterfriend*. This story demonstrates the power of the Holy Spirit to indwell every woman and manifest a miracle.

Sisterfriend, like Mary, we face tremendous challenges. The uncertainty of how God will use us and the possibility of people in our lives not understanding will cause us to have to walk in faith. For comfort, the Holy Spirit will lead us to an Elizabeth who can relate and celebrate with us, because she is pregnant too.

Sisterfriend, something is living within all of us that when birthed could minister to humanity. There is a miracle waiting to come forth in you because you have been chosen, just as Mary. You are *highly favoured*, and God is with you. Make her-story, your-story by believing that God can do the impossible in your life, *and that it will be done unto you, according as He hath said it.*

Christmas

Christmas is the most challenging time of the year for women. It is when mothers feel pressured to buy toys they really can't afford. Wives frantically search for the right gift for the in-laws without help from husbands. Lonely women feel the need to find a man, or hold on to the one they meant to get rid of earlier in the year. The amazing part about all of this is that we will spend January 1st thanking God that it is over, and wake up January 2nd looking forward to it all over again. Despite this contradiction, the challenge is still before us.

Well, I believe it is time to liberate ourselves from this seasonal bondage. Freedom does not come by accident, it has to be planned. My plan is to make this season an expression of what I have to give, and not what someone else wants. Love and attention are the most valuable gifts we can give our children, and it doesn't cost anything. Other family and friends are given fellowship, which never has to be returned because of the wrong color or size. As for the man in, or not in our lives, having a man just to make it through the holidays is like having a temporary job. The benefits are minimal, and you know it is not going to last.

Sisterfriend, remember Christmas is not about how much money you spend, nor is it about swapping gifts with people who already have. It is not even about snuggling with someone on a cold winter's night. Jesus is the reason for the season. He is the greatest gift God gave. Use your freedom in Him to make this season an expression of His love.

Achieving Success

Have you taken the time to seek God's purpose for your life? If so, write it down and post it where you can see it every day. *Write the vision, and make it plain upon tables, that he may run that readeth it. (Hab 2:2).* Having a vision, goal or dream does not require that you know how it is going to be accomplished. Just take the time to get in touch with what's in your heart. Most of the time God's will is hidden in your heart. List your strengths, passions and secret dreams. Talk to people who know you well and get their opinion of your capabilities. Be careful of who you choose to talk with. They should only be people who are positive and aggressive. A person who is stuck in a rut is not going to be too inspiring. Choose friends who are willing to dream with you.

The next step is to establish objectives that are in alignment with your vision. Write them down too. Objectives are smaller goals that will contribute to your ultimate vision. Give yourself a time limit for accomplishing each objective. A time limit is important because it helps you overcome the demon of procrastination.

Now *Sisterfriend*, it's time to put your walking shoes on and hit the pavement. If you desire to go back to school, make application. If it is in your heart to start your own business, develop your business plan.

The soul of the sluggard (lazy) desires and gets nothing, but the soul of the diligent (attentive) is made prosperous (successful) Proverbs 13:4.

Congratulations

We made it, *Sisterfriend!* Another year has come and gone, and we are still here. In spite of the circumstances, through the storm and rain, we endured. Do you realize how much inner strength we possess? We could have given up. We could have allowed life to cause us to surrender our hope. But when times got rough, you and I exposed the *W* for woman, on our chest, and accepted life's challenges. We made meals stretch and ends meet. We comforted others, while sick ourselves. We cared for our children, sometimes being both mother and father. We motivated our husbands and ministered to our friends. We were loyal to our jobs and devoted to our God. Who but a woman of faith could do all that and maintain her sanity?

Sure, we've made some mistakes — who hasn't? And maybe we didn't reach a few goals — who doesn't? The silver lining in the cloud is that if we live to see tomorrow, we will have another opportunity to try again.

So let me be the first to congratulate you for a job well done. If no one else appreciates what you have done, I do. It encourages me to know that Sisters like you still exist. By the way, *Sisterfriend,* God is proud of you also. And you know when He says *well done* blessings are on the way.

25 Ways to Be Good to Yourself

". . . in thy presence is fullness of joy, at thy right hand there are, pleasures forevermore:" Ps. 16:11

1. Exercise
2. Take a bubble bath
3. Read a book
4. Take a day off work (without being sick)
5. Call an old friend
6. Get a massage
7. Buy new makeup and undergarments
8. Rent your favorite movie
9. Give yourself a gift
10. Get a manicure/pedicure
11. Dress up/down for no special reason
12. Try a new hobby
13. Listen to your favorite music
14. Get help with chores around the house
15. Get organized
16. Learn to say no, and not feel guilty
17. Make a new friend
18. Keep a journal
19. Say affirmations every morning
20. Reevaluate your goals
21. Compliment yourself
22. Do something you've never done before
23. Be spontaneous
24. Reserve a daily devotional time
25. Accept love from others

About the Author

Linda Willis is an anointed minister of the Gospel of Jesus Christ.

She is the wife of Rev. Kevin B. Willis, Sr., the mother of Kelli and Kevin, Jr., and the First Lady of Riverside Missionary Baptist Church.

Professionally, Linda is a therapist at Delta Medical Center. She received a Bachelor's of Business Administration Degree at Lemoyne-Owen College and a Master's Degree in Counseling at the University of Memphis.

Linda has published three books entitled *Sisterfriends, Words of Encouragement, Empowerment, and Enlightenment from One Sister to Another* (Volume I & II) *and Pregnant with Potential.*

Linda Willis is a much sought after preacher in the Memphis and surrounding areas. Her source of motivation and strength is found in Matthew 19:26, *With God, all things are possible.*